AF291316

Jacqueline Waters

The Fry

Winter Editions, 2026

Contents

For Leo

Ready for My Statement?

You know I know what I'm doing.
I'm always with you.

I'm watching these lines get to you.
This is how we're close.

We can't have knowing looks
(we're both as good as dead)

so we have these knowing lines,
typing till the clock says stop.

And if in the course of struggle
a foot slips and we fall,

what does that matter?
I won't come back to you

when the song is over.
I will not want you

or your unsuitable house and lot.
Expect to miss me, though—

expect ice and snow, rain and hail.
To be *embarrassed*. To be changed.

To write the year on a check
and be one hundred years off.

To let it go
when I express displeasure.

To let my anger go.
Just drop it.

Just take it
as you drop it, and go.

You Were Grabbed Emotionally

That's not quite it
                either and
        I have to be

honest you guys
                I'm seeing a lot
        of complicated

ideas out there you might say
                it's just me
        conflating ideas

and opinions
                but that piece
        of paper your foot

just totaled
                fell from a table
        that widens

whenever we
                reach across it
        and if too much

has happened
                and you've talked
        too much about it

you have to say
                "never a dull
        moment!"

and with that
            show you regret
        talking about

anything that
            has ever happened
        while inside you

ride like the wind on a horse
            wet with
        sweat the wind also

wet with its own sweat
            the wind
        winds up

and sends a roaring gust
            through the stall
        knocking horses

to their sides
            and humans
        to their knees

and I bet you're asking yourself
            where do we
        go from here?

What's next?
            Well there ought
        to be a set

of kids' measuring tools
            where units get larger
        as the child

abandons the church the yard
                the gully where
        the fern grass grows

as the child
                abandons executive
        business principles

counting cars
                with foreign license plates
        visits to

the child section where everything
                is soft
        angrily outgrowing

softness
                binding oneself
        in hard furnitures

declaring practicality
                in hardness
        while

meeting conspiratorially
                as
        two colleagues

unspooling minute
                after minute
        of appropriate

conversation
                outdoing
        each other

rolling it out
                decisively
        like a truck printing

dashed white lines
                SLOW sign
        on its tail—

just two
                collegial
        enemies

enduring the false conspiracy
                of the shared umbrella
        on a wild, windy night

in the Houlihan's parking lot
                as the child's
        portion grows

*

There should be ritual abandonment of shoes and socks
whenever the church bells sound!

Churches shouldn't get to agitate the air with their
incessant bells!

Nor should they release fragrances with every flip and
flop of the door!

I shouldn't have to duck my head inside my t-shirt every
time I see some kid's parents!

You should be able to reserve picnic tables by turning
them upside down and throwing tomato paste cans—
The park should restrict access to shoes with clear
soles—We ought to be able to drink water all over each
other—We should express longings and yearnings in the
pietà position looking down at the depth of the hope we
don't have—And then there should be voices raised in
complaint—There should be one local mom who breaks
in to tell everyone to cut the shit and say it's time to say
eff you to the people who haven't yet helped us:

Let's say eff you now so they're scared about not
having helped us!

Let's say cut the shit and eff you to these big
institutions meant to instruct us!

Let's get a petition and circulate it to our personal
connections

because there should be an admonition so sharp
so pointed and so precise

that we're breathless at its suitability

or *because* there should be holes in your ideology
giant gaping tears in the garment

revealing your underlying indifference—
indifference like a tattered

rayon lining, or silk batiste, or cotton voile
casting you deep into your little recoils

beside your mini-bitternesses

because they make sense
like everything makes sense

because there's nothing else to make of it

when we come to grips, it's false grips
when we gain an insight it's like we've filled a cart

destined for dispersal
by a thousand years of leg work

*

Dear darling, I woke up today feeling jealous

This is not aimed at anyone
but you know and I know it's YOU

Can you see it all on your own?

Can you solve it
merely with hostility

to its more easily
solvable parts?

*

In the show a character says if you are angry you are a
character in someone else's story

If you get past your anger, you are the protagonist again

They gave that line to a side character
and that makes sense ("like everything makes sense . . .")

*

Then one day you'll
Meet two beavers no one will ever need.
Beaver 1 passes the junction
Pursuant some wood to chew.

Beavers *must* chew wood
To trim their teeth
Or risk teeth
Growing so long
As to pierce their brains.

Anything can happen
was one of our lessons.
But did anyone really learn it.

*

You have emerged from a period of suffering and now
you're ready to prove you're not the person you once
were.

We counted you out, but you've pulled yourself together
and are ready to take back the narrative.

Because there should be a public basin and we should be
made to submerge our arms to the elbows.

And there should be observers with huge pencil tips
pressed into notebooks the size of king-size beds.

And this is not aimed at anyone.

But you know and I know: it's YOU.

Repeat After Me

Let they who thought all that up
enjoy more of that

while I take care of this customer
who may not know I am not

a help line, though I am attentive
to the peculiarities of any problem

anyone calls me over about.
I discover you're alone

and don't like anything around you.
And on the pillow your ear

hears the thunderstorm
straight from the poly-fil.

You've been caught, say by a belt
tightening around your middle

but still you wave
a utensil around

to show right-handedness.
I think it will help

if I repeat after you
without you knowing

your words don't land
but pass over me

like wildly scattered showers.
Then you repeat after me.

When the Geography Was New

No part of the sky
displayed any discernible characteristics

Land, too, lost its recognizable polygons

There was no sound

The only feeling was a powdery scratchiness

There was no one to direct the worker
but there was a rod for gauging width

between two surfaces that fold like a book
which is the reason books exist

to prompt comparison

just as eating anything "like an apple"
means you're a fool

I Wish That Were All, Doctor

Where did you come from?
Why did you come?

Maybe you don't
belong here.

We live in this
wonderful world.

Great flowing fogs
capture our hills

and frosts
whiten our lowlands.

We do not export fruits;
we expect them.

Take this orange.
Push in your chair.

Who has a uniform?
Have I a uniform?

Hush. You are reborn
to people who adore you

and even as fear
contorts your features

your reasoning relies
on a chain of deductions

linking the present
back to a common care.

Joke

Task of getting rhythm
                without adjectives, task
    of throwing verbs around, turning out

two- or three-word phrases
                that open into sold signs
    but without

propositions, like water or mist
                without color behind.
    Proverbs 26:18 calls someone

who deceives you then covers it up
                with *Oh I was only joking*
    a "mad person / hurling death."

All jokes end
                with a heaven sequence
    mostly played offstage

or beneath the curtain
                as it's falling—
    recklessness, passion, delirium

dumped into life
                behind the audience's
    neutral exit.

People Are Work

I am your leader
and I can't answer

without considering
the insipidness

of your need
for instruction

and cataloging it
within my list

of what'll work
to get through a day

with you. The gold
crowns the green

even in these
trembling daffodils

and I know you love me
and you love one another

but I only love you
because I love

my contempt.
Here, your new skills

and there, fleece vest
with one-quarter zip.

You've learned every lover
seeks the other's inspection

that each may tell
the encouraging story

of a life properly inspected.
For now, let's all love

my contempt.
(Don't ever mistake

our fun events
and my fun face.)

A Short History of Who Wants What

So you eat off these plates, most nights, for years.

You got them at Ikea, or they appeared in your cabinet,
inherited from one roommate or another, and each day
you spoon food onto and off of these plates, wash them,
dry them, put them away.

One day you figure out you can take one, press on its
circumference, gather your strength and just ball it back
up into clay.

And then what?

What do you do with the clay?

Hurl it at someone, laughing lightly like it's a snowball
and you're a fun mischievous person, and winter's
everywhere and the stars are flickering.

But it's not winter and you're not light.

You throw your ball the way you practiced, you turn your
back before it lands.

You're Not Full Till Everyone Else Goes Hungry

He says we never paid attention to bells

Never needed to

Our military operates only through the mail

There are twenty-four lessons that take two years to
study

If a student doesn't realize she's unfolding there isn't
much we can do

We'd like to give the lessons for nothing

But we have a growth on our ribs and the only way the
doctors can get it is to saw through six feet of brick

Love feels like all the senses you use during the day relax
and other senses begin to misanthropically surface

That, we don't want

That's an experience
of deprivation

which leads to loitering, "I don't
really need this should I
put it back?" "No. Take its

photo" (she was speaking in a false
whisper)—"To open a store you first

make a list of all the money you're going to lose
Then you start to lose it and feel

right on track"

Interview

Interview begins as soon as you park the car

    Refuse all food and water

Ladies, your voluminous handbag   has no place here

        Focus on accomplishment stories:

"I saved them money by jumping in

      when they needed a nurse | accountant | bouncer"

See what captures the attention   of your practice

    audience

    Use their bathroom and you may as well

      hang a sign around your neck:

UNEMPLOYABLE

Talk only about yourself   let them get used to it

      "People say that I . . ."

      "The great thing about my birth is . . ."

Answer the question behind the question

      Keep answering it   Strip out color

and pictorial representation   Sponge-print what's left

on a strict   middle-class salary

   supplemented by thievery

      and online fundraising

Get Them Out of Here

We should want gods
Curious more of themselves

Ones who take back the onus
And leave us be in our lack

Because maybe the soul *is* the invader
A trespassing, wasteful thing

Happy to overtalk people
Who only ever want to seem

Like they're giving it their all
Counter perceptions of aloofness

While holding
Their richest parts in a place

None of these gods
Get near enough to cheapen

Modern Life Flooded with Lubricating Oils

"Oil is oil" everyone said from the 1850s to the early 1900s
when refiners came up

with all these special-purpose lube oils
and every manufacturer

assigned every machine
its own oil

and it was up to operators to keep track
to shear off the case rivets

turn the connecting posts
and inject a properly

penetrative oil
before the valve handle jammed

or the valve handle snapped
or a hose whipped about violently

And we've got a pilot in our house
Says she got ejected

running through maneuvers
shooting test targets

She parachuted down
like foam-core board on the wind

landed near some farm machinery
no one wants and it rusts

Come get your pilot

Have Another Bite of That John Dory

I tried hard work.
I tried sacrificing things.
Also tried never giving up.

To think I was not fine enough for his generosity.

I was not good enough to wage.

A good meal of fish
fried or prepared any type of way
will nourish you.

Oh and it's nutrients you'll need.
It's nutrients, it's nutrients!
It's always more nutrients you need.

Elbows on the Table

A nurse came in and said it's just too *something*
asserting her moral right
to have an evaluative word supplied . . .

take her advice
and 1,000 units of Vitamin C
1 therapeutic mineral capsule
8 cold boiled shrimp, small or large
bottled cocktail sauce, parsleyed margarine
Who's going to die in here? Maybe that

"VIENNA" tote bag: Freud cartooned
as white sausage
wearing a monocle, "analyzing"
a woman, also sausage, dressed in bloomers
and a Mozart wig
reclining on a wedge
of Sacher-Torte . . .

I'm getting generous
I dream my suitcases are formed of wet clay

and I have to use a shovel
to piece them up and move them to my next room

from there to a hill
where I hunt with a vast field of sons
who trample the depths of my heart, in which

if I listen without lying, I hear
of refreshments bitten with joy:

everything falling together, everyone drumming
a pen on the form
and thinking about how to effectively fill it

The Cool-Off

There's not a lot of food you're best off settling on pumpkin

I'll finish this game
play one more game
and then I'll play you

Then I'll play who's ever called
"next game"

No one here
ought give in to despair

Here is not great

Phones go in a bag

You think you've lost the $20 bill on the way
and you have

What can I tell you?

Here is my help: ________________________

If they used to make thunder
by shaking sheet metal
then what?

Just keep saying it: "I don't care"

That always
exactly works

A Ruse

Couldn't I just
pick up?

Or turn
my hands

face up? You're
as good as shuffled

back into that deck
and I'll miss you

my whole life
if I don't gather up

your egregious silences
and hold them

to my heart
call them love

and care and doting
the way you had to make

consolation out of holes
all the pricks

in your understanding
and the sum

of your uncertainty
steering away the rays

with a high block
to the sun

roundhouse kick
to the bagged-up leaves

and anything I carry
I clasp it close

crush its edges
as I test myself

with your death
which is easily

replenished
or overturned

like any old
open bowl

What Is to Be Done?

You will learn what's done
and you will do it.

Or you will aim to.

Or you will regret
what you've done

also regret the things
you should have done

but didn't do, as well the memories

you might have made
within the love

you should have felt—
"the doorknob off a door and put it back on backward
     softly."

Or do nothing all day
to someone's printout

of a banner ad
for shower steamers.

Neighbor's dog, will it ever stop barking?!

For revenge, record the barks
play them back on speakers

anytime the real-life
barking stops.

(To the world
as noun

what could you
possibly have

to add?)

Watch this video of a river.

Or don't.

I'm not comfortable telling anyone what to do.

You will learn what's done
and you will do it.

It will withdraw from you
whether you accomplish it or not.

The Ancestors (You and Me Both)

I.

I stayed a long while merely to wrest some
higher portion of myself; the remainder went on

worrying and exceeding, racing down a corridor
to beg help of the nuns, waking them

to confirm they feel for me such warmth
it flings them to their feet

they float toward me murmuring
and I eat of a table they prepare

lovingly within my emergency
and their alarm at my distress

is as a balm to me
and surely buttered slices

of a thick brown loaf
and a soup boiled off

their garden's bounty
will make me better

and through me, soothe them, for though
I can see their goodness, I can't see

what makes them good, can't say
it's their aid, for aid is transient

and we tend to regret it
the moment we accept it

I can't say it's their beauty
for they seem to live without it

their table set
with scarred brown plastic

every place cluttered
with evidence of yesterday's repast

and this feeling, I know, is just a branch
of another, more resonant feeling

one that more thoroughly
fills the room

its existence somehow superior
and though I cannot yet contain it

I'm still certain
it would be better off contained

for the sake of either society at large
or me, I can't tell which, and won't

even try, for as long as someone speaks to me
my life is not my own, I am captured

in the timidity of my response
which no longer emerges automatically

but must be set in motion
by a gear wheel so weakened I hesitate

to position it against the others, lest they all
push each other to pieces

II.

A world ought to be clear, and instructional
providing parts for each participant to sing

into a harmony suitable for shelving angels in the eaves
and it ought to be vague enough

to appeal to anyone searching
for a strong supporting argument

(here I conflate vagueness with strength
for neither interrogates the other)

and anyone arriving in their bathrobe
ought to reconsider the sense

that anything is so close
as to be part you

and I'll be solemn
if indicated, or shout the name of the city we're in

with a human's way of knowing
how big or small to go

raising a name in praise . . .
for I need to be moved

every day by some truly motivating verse
convincing no one of its anonymity

but hounding me like I hound
and feel it as hounding

meaning I feel like a hound—
a smart, aspiring hound

and not your child given
the collar, the tag, the name

III.

Nobody took the blame, finally
and nobody would

Blame stalled
like a feather in some
area of unusual pressure

I have to talk like this because the faucet is on

I have to talk at least as well as a faucet

What little have we felt
for one another

Let's get it all sacked up

Let's get you out of here

The Fry

The devil said:
Remember me.

And I said:
We're a pair.

We're a twosome
and a duo

and I'll obey
should you ever

give an order.
OK.

Tell them
you fucking hate them.

Advise them love
is obedience

to the nick of time
as you flatten

your chest
against it: the nick

the almost-not
forever.

A little fly
in your lunchbox?

You're not afraid.
You can crush it

in the plies
of a napkin.

Sounds in the plumbing?

You're not afraid!

It's you for whom

the republic learns

its vows . . .

I mean don't you think

what struck you as insight

(your own) when you said

(to your friend), *I wasn't sleeping*

because there was

too much light

in the apartment

might have been just a PAWING

    at connection—that you aren't

        SOCIALIZED unless you agree

    happenings have CAUSES

aren't just SUCCESSIVE

    related one to the other

      like a royal family

    and just as LILY-LIVERED?

    *

Is your hat
flung to a kitchen chair?

Is it noon?

Companions,
what do you think?

Have we had enough
of those soaring eagles?

Have we had enough
of those trumpets?

Go on, thoughts

Go on
like a hammering

in the upstairs
apartment

rhythmically
nonsensical

yet staking
efficacy

on a recurring
sense of

"Surprise!
It's me again!"

I'm here
to hit

each word
out of your

head send it
sailing on

the wind
toward

the family eating
in its own

plexiglass box
attentive only

to the server's
basket of bread

and burnt-up
bowl of oil

Sash the Winner

How no one is given enough of that or of love
and it ekes out through the speeches

And what about the tears?

Oh, if you hold your eyes open long enough
they come down your face

Contrite the Winner

I shouldn't be so hard
I should be lovely and soft

I shouldn't daydream about their faces
taking my punches

mopping up lost blood
with a damp rag

wringing out the rag
to water my houseplants

She is in the crossing now
I am in the crossing too

I am trying to draw a dotted line
around all my anger
so they can cut it out

We're surgeons! We can help!

It will be good for you to inform us
where you *hope to communicate*
and where you *plan to be interpreted*

The Right Tool for the Job

"yeah I've never been able to keep a secret I have a lack
of deceptive experience . . . I can only keep up with a
conspiracy theory if I'm also conspiring in my everyday
life . . . like if I take my dog off leash in the park against
the rules, but in collusion with the other owners with
whom I stand and trade raw dog food recipes . . . dangle
a knotted rope at my dog then throw it . . . watch as
my dog eats from the plates of picnickers . . . sniffs at
the diaper of a baby . . . knocks the baby over with its
nose . . . and I see this and say to my friends, 'hang on a
moment—it involves raw beef, toasted oats, and young
apple—but hang on, I've got to handle this' . . . and I
yell my dog's name loud for show . . . as the mother of
the knocked-over baby who is mostly consumed with
comforting the baby, also turns to ravage me—me!
innocent dog owner—with a lot of sharp words you have
to laugh at in the mouth of a mother . . . and you have to
say 'calm down, lady' . . . because who else will say it? . . .
'calm down, lady, the baby's fine' . . . and you shouldn't
have a baby in this park anyway . . . I'm going to call the
cops about your baby . . . cops love recipes with spirulina
and creatine . . . and nootropics for more powerful and
inquisitive dogs . . . cops are on the side of animals . . .
babies are afraid to take sides . . . and fear is what's wrong
with this world . . . imagine letting anyone's curiosity
knock you over . . . and being offended by that? . . .
how about you get a more stable baby . . . maybe learn a
little about the obliques . . . core is important . . . you've
got to believe in the core if you're going to do anything
about life . . . obliques help you turn sideways if you
have to . . . but mainly they keep everything straight . . .

straight is the best . . . dogs that eat industrial dog food are clowns . . . I'm shutting this down soon . . . if you're having any trouble with your computer call me . . . if any part of your setup bothers you I can take a look"

Laundromat

    —but once or twice a year

they also wash a comforter, shoving it alone

    into the largest machine, selecting "extra rinse"

    ensuring no residue

clings to the feathers

of the birds abandoned inside: notice now

    a few people

circled up near the dryers

    distracting me while I try to read

    a short story that (coincidentally)

takes place in a laundromat

where I always have

    these business ideas

mentally selecting

    a list of colleagues

    convincing them we have a secret

making sure everyone senses

the secret's perimeter: who's in, who's out

    until customers pick up

on the attunement energy

    emanating from what is now

    a group of hyperconnected colleagues

pressing their shoulders

metaphorically

    to the same door

and clients find themselves

    responding with complete agreement

    reaching with the coffee pot

over the conference table

asking if there is anyone more they can pour for

    and suddenly we have it: *authority*

which we wield, as you would imagine

    with great reason and care

and maybe it's a trick, but it's not

a scam exactly, and anyway maybe

what we call authority is just

    an invitation to engage

with a banquet of intriguing

    asymmetries, as though authority—

    real authority—were an art

and I may as well say

the most important kind of art

    is cautionary art

especially the kind that cautions you

    against enjoying

    any other kind of art

warning you of art's tendency to disarm you

or to turn you into

    a dissembler—for we all make apologies

through our values

which are themselves apologies

for an insincere relationship with gold

or gold futures, or luminous

gold jewelry or golden pails

of buckwheat honey

gold-covered chia seeds

spilling in golden sunlight

filaments of spun gold pressed into blank cakes

the size of tractor wheels—

though the moral's the same:

we have a duty to our souls

for we have preferred our souls dependent

and duty is not a *show*—

if I give you a system

for behaving well

and an audience

to observe and guide your use of it

and also specialists

    to mark your progress

    plus a family to compliment

the bounty you bring them, then

it's like I was *always* even, never shaken

    always *upstanding*—

never wrapped in a comforter

    and rolled down a levee—

    always with a *smile*, never biting

the odd end

of a pencil—and always up

    for anything, never smacked

with a mackerel-shaped potholder

    but rather forever ready

    to prep a snack tray

chalk up a misgiving

overlook an absence

dramatize a dressing room conflict

wrap up early, offer to stay late

fast unto death, rise

from the dead, propose

wholesome penalties, overwhelm the old, point out

you're shrinking in fear

from what you know to be right—

my boy tells me if ever he gets a dog

it will be a golden retriever

so it can retrieve gold

and as it rolls over on him

in its sleep, this dog, gold spills

from its jaws:

ingots and medallions, rocks with veins

clumps of golden lattice cereal

crushed and pressed into his shoes

like a crumb crust

in a pie shell—

    everyone had one, "a great idea"

and if you didn't have one

    people thought you were crazy

    or that you just

had had a bad night's sleep and you *did* have one—

we slow gold, source of all good

    down to its terrible essence

a form of declining

    self-regard

    or increased foreign competition

overtly overflowing—

and though the conclusion I reached

    may have had more to do

with actions I was already

    inclined toward than any

    skill at interpretation

I possessed, nonetheless

my take proved popular:

  "When you put it like that . . ."

was a phrase I heard a lot

  over the next few hours

  as the sun sank

on our very own

local laundromat

for Brian Kalkbrenner

Oh You Found the Old Home Movies

That's it? A power plant and a half-built baseball park?

I'm not sure I *can* be hypnotized

We go in a little

cloud cover

We go in nothing

You wouldn't need to hypnotize *me* to do that

We go in after them

with these tongs

You, for one, take responsibility

Jump right up for some idea

but *refuse* to repeat

any of the words it arrived in

or *challenge* yourself

to repeat all the words while

managing to alter slightly

the idea—which if I could find it

I'd like to find it in the trash

unfold and smooth it

know from one word ("humility")

that I'd discovered an intimacy

torn into fourths

each fourth stacked

in heart-pounding order

Us 'n' Nature

We didn't love fragrant petals awfully much

Beasts we couldn't create ongoing connection with

Pelts had beauty but we weren't interested in collecting

Most determinations we would have been OK if they were
never made

Truly it was all an experiment in continuing to have a
good time at everyone else's expense

Could you stop tending to strangers?

Could you let a badly prepared meal fall out of your
mouth, back onto the paper plate, while conveying
confidence in the uncorroborated petitioner?

Gone are the days of leaching lye out of wood ashes

Each morning we list our grudges in a note then delete
the note

At the end of the week we read through all our deleted
notes until we're furious enough to overturn a freshly laid
table which we do

People wait more calmly when they know everyone else
has also been waiting everywhere, from forever ago, and
their waits have counted nothing toward a guarantee of a
future end to the wait

We haven't put
a historical plaque on it yet, she says

Just this laminated sign reading
"Please do not climb

on this artifact. It is
not safe."

Choosing a Language for Your Project

It's OK, I'll use my old data here to grab some new,
similar data, with similarity determined by a pasta
puttanesca

built by a machine trained to run after long shots
and shoot sharpened car parts, collateral piled up

in grooves along the side like the bumpers
you turn on for kids on the bowling trip

(Bowling trip's only for honor roll; secrecy surrounds
the permission slip)

There's no trace of gray in the acrylic set
No set of eyes in the nails

No, you should not seek shelter under an overpass
in a tornado, nor should you join your neighbor in a
crawlspace

neither of you controls
You are trying to cause a scene

but the fog in here is hiding
your outrageous behavior

Friends, the mind finds all
unless you strongly halt it

Oh You Found the Old Home Movies II

When you have forgotten it all, is that when bare feet on
grass feels fulfilling and not like nausea of the foot?

I'm told I've been dissociating, which is when your mind
goes to make a sandwich while your body continues
as the bread in someone else's larger, more important
sandwich . . .

When your child acts out: think have you dashed a
plan to drill your friends in love of chores set to music
composed by mentors in incomplete behavior . . .

Behavior is communication and if you find it a strain
to behave well then you might consider italics or
<blockquote> tags around your sulking and a large
hero image above your swipe at another child's tower of
stacked vacuum bags . . .

Remember, each of us develops our own communication
system . . .

Observe your child's system carefully in case it may be
patented . . .

Or plagiarized . . .

You learn by doing, you thrive by owning . . .

Five or more portions of finger food a week and you'll
show less fear as you crumple toddlers against the
cubbies to hoard the magnet tiles . . .

Don't be in a hurry to be so independent . . .

Losers aren't likely to ask permission to bury the game
ball in a bag of yogurt-covered mini-men . . .

In a sought-after menstrual schedule . . .

In a diamond pile at a mine-your-own-diamond mine . . .

Score is 8 plagued by 4 . . .

Decimal point punctures the otherwise pristine analysis
of the dying actuary . . .

Bend the stick and rotate the paddles . . .

I can be real about this latest twist in the mix-up, right?

By the time I got it right I had already had it wrong so
often I decided to get on board with every wrong thing I
heard from then on out . . .

This is the way form loosens . . .

Having painted the handles a choked-out pink . . .

Like eternity never came along in anything but loss . . .

None of this loss lasted, but we ask it last . . .

Ask it last, then complain it lasts too long . . .

What Might Good Be

Everyone just relax

This operation's not what you think

We don't use sharp instruments

Barely do we cut

Our observations are done at home in our heads

We push you around while you sleep

Then we send all your junk to the lab

The lab woman gets all this junk

And says she's sorry but it's mostly uninteresting

Then we all let you go

Further into the mystery

"Don't fear the treatment, fear the disease"

Fear and keep fearing

Your fear is like a cold hot tub someone keeps suggesting
you sit in

There's nowhere else to sit

Nowhere else to be

So it's back in the tub with you

*

What would you like?

—Just anything that has no worth beyond meaning

or the thought that counts when gifted

(fork poking

the accumulated ham)

*

Hello! I have designed your treatment

Sit here and I'll dump in some powders

Radio says rain today

It wasn't my responsibility to save you but I did it

You're like my little doll

I can tell you'd like to move everyone over

To your way of thinking

We cost the same shadows

Why not

Think the same thoughts?

For what, exactly, might good be?

Might it be wisdom

Tipping innocence

Off the mantel?

One team hunts for it in the bones of your ear

Another team walks the length of your torso, roping off
squares for study

Someone finds a brush and pan, begins to go through the
waves in your hair

A worry is just an explanatory adjective such as *moral* or
horizontal

You keep having to pay everyone

A technician readies her magical wand

You pay for the wand time, the magic, the gel

You pay extra to warm up the gel

Security runs their checks then hands you Patient swipe

Patient swipe nonfunctional they hand you Visitor swipe

Eventually a voice is raised at the back of the room

Eventually a cloud ices up and drops like rock on a pack
of nested airport carts

Stacks of nested tumblers, towers of nested bowls, fall
over: nests lost

And I did mean to teach you

But you could not align with my knowledge:

Every surety, every certainty

Rests, by necessity, on an ignorance

This ignorance must be renewed and replenished

Lower your bowl down deep in the water

Shout it with me: we are crossing over!

We are crossing over by breaking our fear of depths off
of us

I'm supplying you this costly bottle of finishing oil

Anoint with it and watch my word order here

Anoint you yourself with great specificity

To the earliest part of your body

To your body's first and now most anointed part

*

Guys, she is fine, it's no big deal

God rode each molecule of poison produced from
the yew tree down through her chest port into the
appropriate chamber of her heart

also sent the echocardiography team of Lenox Hill
to check it behind a curtain in a hallway every three
months

and let those specialists complain about her scars
how those and the implants impeded their view

let them sigh and push harder
and they knew it would hurt and had them tell her so

and they groaned and dug their wand between her ribs
trying to get an image at Position 7

so they wouldn't be in trouble
with the supervisor on call

and God told them not to care any extra here
that it would be best to do the minimum and move on

and when she asked for maybe an ice pack God was in
their ear

instructing them No no no, this is where you refuse!

THIS IS WHERE YOU ARE RIGHTEOUS IN REFUSAL
OF EXTRA

Yes, her heart opened and closed each day

The opening was God and the closing was her fault

God lifted her up!

We were good in our praise and our worship
for God had gotten tough with us

gathered us up in the KFC parking lot
and gave us instructions and cover

"I lay this all now on your shoulders
and it flows one to the other like a rope

a thousand pounds of rope
or heavy hose

like when a plane's hit a skyscraper
and the *NY Post* thinks it's a good idea for you to go in
there

to inspect every floor that will fall on you"

(Look at their faces, how they look when they
believe it's good and right you go through with it
that you take all the pain—and they push)

Seriously guys she is fine

She is grateful to God who gets all the glory for her
miraculous recovery

The doctors were all men and they were intelligent and
exacting!

The nurses all women and they brought tough love and
courtesy!

God paid all the bills, her sisters and brothers surrounded
her with love and concern

Their love lifted the hearts of her family!

    CURTAIN

       *

People are your human mirrors

If you don't like how you see yourself in one of them it
makes sense to spend the afternoon criticizing them for
their humorlessness

Really rake them over the coals

Someone has to believe in justice and turn their head
from a mess

People don't want other people's mushroom vegan
meatloaf

Mouths don't want other mouths

Bereaved don't want to move on to drinks when the
speaker's finished

Ill don't want you to stop contacting them in the guise of
guarding their privacy

Grace doesn't want to be said

Let alone had

Let's none of us measure

The depth of any particular congratulations

Confetti, let it be where it fell

Believe every being is granted the exact same amount

Of "good" and "bad" feelings over a lifetime

Just with different units for those amounts

Different shapes for those units

Alternative vocabularies in the letters

Suggesting you exit the premises

*

You forget that I know you

You have no imagination that I'm not monitoring

Have no depiction I'm not regretting

You move through life with your chin on the tablecloth
while others add up the check

I'm angry at them for insisting on pretending none of this
is happening

And when I say so she says everyone has problems not
just you

What are your problems   how are you tending them
where do they go without you

We are just your family you cannot expect us to notice
you

Your expectations here are the problem

Reduce those and you'll be back having fun on the group
text

You'll like the photo of the first day of school

You'll like everything about it so you'll like it over and over

Its orange light filling your sinuses, sparks springing out
of your eyes

Igniting the eyebrows you're lucky are about to fall out
anyway

"Try eyebrow lamination"

"Try eyebrow transplant"

"Try holding your head close to a person with good
eyebrows"

*

I admire the rubberized chain pull

And touch it when they turn their back

Pull it when they leave

Sometimes I drink their water

And when they go to drink it

There is nothing left

You don't understand that time accumulates

Without satisfying itself

So that the people you left

To fend for themselves

Cause you to close a door on yourselves . . .

Therefore we act extremely when we die, we make dust,
because we intend to blow back our footprints, pressed
thoughtlessly along the earth, and our footprints, which
the world intends to blow itself free of, we circle up
around and tend, we go back and we try to make them,
to the living, plain to see . . .

It's like a foot, socked, on a metal measuring plate . . .

It's like I'm almost not here, but I still have to show ID . . .

It's like will call is a place and not a pronouncement . . .

For I think I saw a well

I know I saw a concrete slab

I don't know how thick it was, but every time he sang
that song it began to crack in the middle

Similarly we sing

That there will be a striking down of every obstacle

And now you are removing the restriction on my right
ankle

The snake wrapped around it

Is now crushed

Venom injected in my blood system

Is considered removed

Surgeon is saying, I am withdrawing all the drama

Going back three or four years now

I am restoring you to this hour

I am reseating you

People who would not fulfill the assignment, I am ejecting
them

Wiping their crumbs off chairs for you

Your season of loss is over

Go ahead and bronze the hinge of the door that you
could not get through

Make your own little keepsakes and monuments

Sometimes you must persevere without knowing what
you're doing or even shouting

You ring the victory bell the loudest

Everyone smiling hollers and laughs because you reached
into a lion's mouth to do it

The lion bit but the bite was soft

Teeth like ladyfingers

No you cannot be invisible it's never OK

You have to get in their faces like even their turtleneck
elastic's weak

Those still in our care will have their updates posted to
the monitor

If you see a green square illuminated go search for a
person to retrieve

Acknowledgments

I am grateful to the publications where versions of these poems first appeared: *Big Bell*, *Chicago Review*, *Critical Inquiry*, *Harper's Magazine*, the Academy of American Poets' Poem-a-Day series, and Lorraine Lupo's Periodic Postcard project. My gratitude as well to Little Pink Houses of Hope.

JACQUELINE WATERS is the author of three previous books of poetry: *Commodore* and *One Sleeps the Other Doesn't*, both from Ugly Duckling Presse, and *A Minute Without Danger*, published by Adventures in Poetry. Her work has appeared in *Chicago Review*, *Harper's Magazine*, the PEN Poetry Series, and on Poets.org. Born in Jersey City, New Jersey, she lives in New York City and works on the digital team at Lincoln Center for the Performing Arts.

ISBN 978-1-959708-18-6

First Edition, 2026 — 1200 copies

Winter Editions, Brooklyn, New York
wintereditions.net

Library of Congress Control Number: 2026932093

Distributed by Asterism Books (US) and Public Knowledge (UK)

Typeset in Heldane, a renaissance-inspired serif designed by Kris Sowersby for Klim Type Foundry, and Zirkon, a contemporary gothic designed by Tobias Rechsteiner for Grilli Type. Design based on series templates developed in consultation with Andrew Bourne.

This book was printed and bound in Lithuania by BALTO print with Munken papers. Manufactured by Arctic Paper in Sweden, Munken meets EU Ecolabel, Forest Stewardship Council, and Cradle to Cradle certification standards.

WE is grateful for the support of our subscribers, and extends special thanks to recent Supporting and Lifetime Subscribers: Anonymous (2), Anonymous (in memory of the Beaubiens), Yevgeniy Fiks, and Katy Lederer.

WE is a member of the Community of Literary Magazines and Presses (CLMP) and of Poetry Corp., a publishing cooperative. Tax-deductible donations are much appreciated and should be made through our fiscal sponsor, Ether Sea Projects, Inc.

 Winter Editions

Emily Simon, IN MANY WAYS

Garth Graeper, THE SKY BROKE MORE

Robert Desnos, NIGHT OF LOVELESS NIGHTS, tr. Lewis Warsh

Richard Hell, WHAT JUST HAPPENED

Marina Tëmkina & Michel Gérard, BOYS FIGHT

Claire DeVoogd, VIA

Monica McClure, THE GONE THING

Ahmad Almallah, BORDER WISDOM

Hélio Oiticica, SECRET POETICS, tr. Rebecca Kosick

Heimrad Bäcker, DOCUMENTARY POETRY, ed. & tr. Patrick Greaney

Robert Fitterman, CREVE COEUR

Karla Kelsey, TRANSCENDENTAL FACTORY: FOR MINA LOY

Alan Gilbert, THE EVERYDAY LIFE OF DESIGN

Betsy Fagin, FIRES SEEN FROM SPACE

Cristina Pérez Díaz, FROM THE FOUNDING OF THE COUNTRY

Sarah Riggs, LINES

Leah Flax Barber, THE MIRROR OF SIMPLE SOULS

Monique Wittig, THE LESBIAN BODY, tr. David Le Vay

Monique Wittig, ACROSS THE ACHERON, tr. David Le Vay with Margaret Crosland

Nathalie Quintane, THE CAVALIER, tr. Jonathan Larson

Serena Solin, A BARER SKY

James Loop, METRONOME

Jacqueline Waters, THE FRY

Iliassa Sequin, QUINTETS, ed. Luke Roberts

Keith Newton, REVOLUTIONS AMONG US

Jean Day, THE ELEMENTS

Rodrigo Toscano, SALVAGE NATION

POSTCARDS OF THE SIEGE: VISUAL CULTURE DURING THE SIEGE OF LENINGRAD (1941–1944), ed. Polina Barskova

Vasily Kamensky, TANGO WITH COWS, tr. Eugene Ostashevsky, ed. Daniel Mellis